Northamptonshire

Edited by Donna Samworth

First published in Great Britain in 2007 by:
Young Writers
Remus House
Coltsfoot Drive
Peterborough
PE2 9JX
Telephone: 01733 890066
Website: www.youngwriters.co.uk

SB ISBN 978-1 84602 958 5

Foreword

Young Writers was established in 1991 and has been passionately devoted to the promotion of reading and writing in children and young adults ever since. The quest continues today. Young Writers remains as committed to the nurturing of poetic and literary talent as ever.

This year's Young Writers competition has proven as vibrant and dynamic as ever and we are delighted to present a showcase of the best poetry from across the UK and in some cases overseas. Each poem has been selected from a wealth of *Little Laureates* entries before ultimately being published in this, our sixteenth primary school poetry series.

Once again, we have been supremely impressed by the overall quality of the entries we have received. The imagination, energy and creativity which has gone into each young writer's entry made choosing the poems a challenging and often difficult but ultimately hugely rewarding task - the general high standard of the work submitted ensured this opportunity to bring their poetry to a larger appreciative audience.

We sincerely hope you are pleased with this final collection and that you will enjoy *Little Laureates Northamptonshire* for many years to come.

Contents

Long Buckby Junior School

Oakway Junior School

Nathan Carter (8)   59
Annabella Costantino (9)   59

Pitsford Primary School
Emily Reed (7)   60
Joshua Jess (9)   61
Lucy Richmond (7)   62
Chloe Cooper (8)   63
Meg Bamford (9)   64
Charlie Lloyd (7)   64
Olivia Bott (8)   65
Huw Redwood (8)   65
Abigail Biggs (8)   66
Daniel Collins (8)   67

Ringstead CE Primary School
Matthew Chamberlain (7)   67
Frances Talman (8)   68
Ellie Defries (7)   68
Gemma Hollis (7)   69
Alec Morgan (8)   69
Tom Watton (8)   70
Benn Martin (8)   70
Jack Palmer (10)   71
William Westall (11)   71
Andy Lees (10)   72
Katie Surridge (11)   72
Gemma Horton (11)   73
Natalie De Quincey-Wykes (8)   73
Christian Brigginshaw (11)   74
Thomas Lees (9)   74
Michael Towers (10)   75

St Mary's CE Primary School, Burton Latimer
Ryan Lacey (11)   75
Ethan Field (9)   75
Kade Purbrick (10)   76
Chloe Baugh (10)   76
Annie Wilkinson (10)   76
Elena Attfield (11)   77
Hannah Rose (11)   77

Maisy Smith (11)   77
Alysha Kassam (9)   78
Adam Tattersdale (10)   78
Danielle Reeve (11)   79
Hannah Gurney (9)   79
Layla Lindsay (10)   79
Anne Grey (10)   80
Conor Sellers (10)   80
Jacob Bryan (9)   80
Andrew Winebrenner (11)   81
Taylor Robinson (10)   81
Danielle Evans (10)   81
Nicholas Shelford (10)   82
James Southcombe (10)   82
Matthew Bull (9)   82
Caprice Bale (9)   83
Corina Bulita (9)   83
Laura Ross (9)   83
Katherine Davies (10)   84
Joseph Harpur (10)   84
Charley Hull (10)   84
Joanna Chandler (9)   85
Abigail Hillyard (9)   85
Makayla Rettie (9)   85
Dannielle Ives (11)   86
Emily Hall (11)   86
Jordan Anniwell (10)   86
Aidan Cunningham (9)   87
Benjamin Mitchell-Bunce (9)   87
Libby Wood (11)   87
Mary Stone (9)   88
Charlotte Watkins (10)   88

St Mary's CE (VA) Primary School, Kettering
Jack Shipton (11)   88
Nathan Carr (11)   89
Elliott Gillies (11)   89
Courtney Searle (11)   90
Kuldeep (11)   90
Philomena Besa (11)   90
Tom Bates (10)   91

Charles Angus (10)	91
Jamie Cooper (10)	91
Sonia Bali (10)	92
Chloe Kingston (10)	92
Chelsea Lewis (10)	93

Tiffield CE (VA) Primary School

Alistair Ferrie (9)	93
George Oddy (9)	94
Charlie Brammer (10)	94
Tom Hunt (10)	95
William Wilkins (10)	95
Rona Ireland (9)	96
Joseph Pady (9)	96
Andrew Hopes (10)	97

Welford, Sibbertoft & Sulby Endowed Primary School

Fred Highton (10)	97
Joe Todd (9)	98
Sam Baylis (10)	98
William Rhodes (9)	99
Georgia Bennett (10)	99
Francesca Lansdell (9)	99
Megan Short (9)	100
William Boulton (10)	100
Sarah Cliffe (10)	101
Amanda Wallace (10)	101
Harrison Coltman (9)	102
Anthony Banks (9)	102
Megan Towers (9)	103
Mark Hansford (8)	103
Harriet Cant (9)	104
Georgia Jones (10)	104

Welton CE Primary School

Mathew Gay (10)	105

West Haddon Primary School

Eleanor Bickers (10)	106
Georgia May (9)	107

The Poems

Snow

Icy crystals floating
Through the air.
Snow! Snow! Snow!
Like little men parachuting
Out of a cloud.
Snow! Snow! Snow!
Shows us things
From not long ago.
Snow! Snow! Snow!
Like a giant's
White blanket.
Snow! Snow! Snow!
Like a ball of ice cream
From the freezer.
Snow! Snow! Snow!
Melting so quickly
Spring is coming.

Harry Moir (9)
Beachborough School

Snow

I can see the snow floating, fluttering,
From the dark clouds in the sky.
On the floor a white blanket lies
Silently, untouched.
As I take my first steps,
The snow crunches beneath my feet.
The sun comes out from behind the clouds,
The snow starts to turn to slush.
The frozen ponds start to melt,
The ice skaters are going home.

Georgia Alderton (9)
Beachborough School

Snow

I look outside
The snow looks like a blanket
And clouds look like pillows or tiny marshmallows.
The steeple is white,
It is such a pretty sight.
I walk outside.
Crunch, crunch.
The pond is frozen,
The ducks cannot swim.
I walk outside.
Stars inside stars
Like little things from Mars.
I've looked outside.
Crunch, crunch.

Sacha Percival (9)
Beachborough School

Snow

Snowflakes silently gliding,
They look like mini parachutes,
As they silently fall to the ground.
When they land you just want to eat them,
They look like icing on a cake.
As you step on the snow it is so slushy,
But when the sun comes out
The blanket of snow goes away.

Zoë Amos (9)
Beachborough School

Snow

Snow is like crystal,
Glistening in the sun.
Snow is like ice cream,
Slushy and cold.
Snow is as white as a sheet
When you wake up
In the morning.
Snow is like
The icing on a cake.
Snow drifts silently
Down from the sky.
Snow is as icy
As the roads in the morning.
That is snow!

Hebe Richardson (10)
Beachborough School

Snow

Snow is as white as a sheet,
Snow is beautiful, falling from the sky.
Snowflakes fall from the clouds.
Snowflakes are very cold.
The ponds and lakes are frozen,
Covered with snow.
Snow is cold.
The snow is melting,
Here comes spring,
Goodbye snow.

Dhillon Smart (10)
Beachborough School

My Outer Space Box

(Based on 'Magic Box' by Kit Wright)

I would put in my box . . .
The twinkle of the marvellous Milky Way,
When the dark of night appears
And the vast black hole,
That sucks in unsuspecting spaceships.

I would put in my box . . .
All the planets, big and small,
From balls of fiery flame
To the smallest rocks
Spinning around the sun.

I would put in my box . . .
The magical swirling of the moons,
Roaming around the super planet master,
From nothing, in a few seconds,
To the magnificent boom of the Big Bang.

My box is made of
Moon dust, covered in an asteroid belt
Floating in zero gravity
Frozen in time
Padlocked with a boiling sun key.

Devon Berrington (10)
Beachborough School

Snow

A white sheet has fallen on top of the small mountain
And the cold winter breeze
Has frozen the drops of the great Trevi fountain.
The world has turned white over the night,
While we are tucked up in bed
Nice and tight.

Jonathon Carter (10)
Beachborough School

The Fun Box

(Based on 'Magic Box' by Kit Wright)

I will put in my box . . .
The windy seaside
And the sandcastles two feet high
The jokes of my best friends
That makes our sides ache.

I will put in my box . . .
The steam and bubble
Of hot chocolate,
And an old book
With crumpled yellow pages.

I will put in my box . . .
A massive Lego brick city
And my colourful
Silly drawings.

I will put in my box . . .
The laughter of children playing,
My archery bow
With its shining limbs
And beautiful handle.

Ralph Buzzoni (10)
Beachborough School

Snow

I see icy, glistening snow in the morning.
Cold snow! Cold snow! Cold snow!
Slushy snow glittering down from the treetops.
Sparkling ice! Sparkling ice! Sparkling ice!
The snow is melting now,
Come spring! Come spring! Come spring!

Edward Nixon (10)
Beachborough School

My Sport Box

(Based on 'Magic Box' by Kit Wright)

I will put in my box . . .
The cheer of the crowd
When England score a goal
The tactics of Rooney
And the skill of Beckham
The football from the first World Cup
And the numerous goals.

I will put in my box . . .
The stroke of Kevin Pietersen
The throw of Strauss
And the crash of the stumps
When the ball hits home.

I will put in my box . . .
The crack of the hockey stick
When I score a goal
The smash of the glass
When playing in the garden.

I will put in my box . . .
The shouts of the supporters
When England won the World Cup
The scream of pain
From Jonny Wilkinson when he was injured
The cries of Australia
When they lost the game.

My box is made of
The leather of Thierry Henry's boots,
It is lined with the turf
From the Emirates Stadium.
And is locked with the key
From the World Cup trophy cabinet
Opened only by winners.

Edward Arnold (10)
Beachborough School

My Supercar Box

(Based on 'Magic Box' by Kit Wright)

In my box I will put . . .
The revving V10 engine
Speeding the Ferrari along
The pistons being put to the test
Powering the Zonda along

In my box I will put . . .
The sleek lines of a Lamborghini
Blowing the minds of pedestrians
And the low aerodynamic roof
With the breeze rushing over

In my box I will put . . .
The fresh skidmarks
Of a drifting car spinning around
And the rush of air
As the Porsche zooms by

My box is made of
Carbon fibre car parts
Shaped to perfection
And it is locked with the speedometer
Of the Mclaren F1.

Joseph Cooney (10)
Beachborough School

Snow

They drift, they glide,
Cold, slushy, crunchy.
White sheets of it fall and rest,
They fall like a white blanket of crystals, glistening.
Snow is here at last
And with it comes winter and fun!

Tobias Sneyd-Garrity (9)
Beachborough School

My US Sports Box

(Based on 'Magic Box' by Kit Wright)

I would put in my box . . .
The RFK stadium
To watch the Nationals anytime I choose
The sound of the bat cracking when it is hit for a home run
The cry of the empire
'You're out!'
The roar of the crowd
'We want a pitcher, not a belly itcher!'

I would put in my box . . .
Santana Moss
From the Washington Redskins
I would take his jersey
And treasure it forever

I would put in my box . . .
The Washington Wizards
So I can get autographs and tickets
Gilbert Arenas would have game-winning 3 pointers
The cheering of the crowd
And the sweat from the players
As it drains down their faces

My box would be made of
An old trophy case
That held many famous cups
It is tied with old basketball laces
And buried in the middle of a baseball diamond.

Evan Kalaris (11)
Beachborough School

My Simpsons' Box

(Based on 'Magic Box' by Kit Wright)

I will put in my box . . .
The sound of Krusty's chokey shout
As Sideshow Mel gets blown out of a cannon
The cry of Homer when the Duff bear
And doughnuts are out of stock
And also the devil of Bart

I will put in my box . . .
The evil eyes of Sideshow Bob
The dirtiness of Nelson's boring clothes
And the relationship between Principle Skinner
And Mrs Krabapple

I will put in my box . . .
The busy hair of Marge
The appetite of Chief Wiggan
And the oldness of Hans Moleman

My box is made out of chewy, salty hot dogs
And the evil laugh of old Monty Burns
It is wrapped in the cat skin of poor Snowball
1, 2 and 3!

Edward Measey (11)
Beachborough School

Snow

I woke up in the morning
There wasn't a sound.
I looked out of the window and found
Snowflakes drifting and gliding
To form a blanket of snow.
It looked slushy.
I went outside.
It was all icy and the snow was untouched.
Snow, snow, I like snow!

Elizabeth Treadwell (10)
Beachborough School

My Horse Box

(Based on 'Magic Box' by Kit Wright)

I will put in my box . . .
My first canter in the winter breeze
The smell of hay
And a beautiful shire horse
Who, in the blink of an eye, disappears.

I will put in my box . . .
A grooming brush
Lost in a fire years ago
And the jump of the thoroughbred
As he crosses the finishing pole.

I will put in my box . . .
The bridle of a pony
Who passed away saving a little girl
The sweet nickering of a lost soul
And the pound of hooves as they stop time's tick.

I will put in my box . . .
The Polos found in a stable
Before it closed forever
And the beat of a heart from within.

My box will be made of
Horseshoes found in a forest
And a tossed mane
It will be lined with the sorrow
Of little girls whose ponies have passed
It will be locked with the strength
Of a whip and can only be opened
With a magic spell of time.

Jenna Rowe (11)
Beachborough School

My Military Box

(Based on 'Magic Box' by Kit Wright)

I will put in my box . . .
The Tomahawk gliding
Sneakily through the sky
In stealthy silence
And the 808 rifle
Firing deadly shots
At the enemy.

I will put in my box . . .
The cry of triumph
When William the Conquer
Won the Battle of Hastings
And the scream of death
When Harold got shot in the eye.

I will put in my box . . .
The luger that shot Adolph Hitler
The power of the Atomic bomb
The daring of the Japanese navy
When they attacked Pearl Harbour.

My box is made of titanium
The trim is lined with arrow tips and bullets
And the lock would be trinnium
With a one million lock number key pad
And if it was opened
Then history would repeat itself
But twice as long.

Charlie Mason (11)
Beachborough School

My Terror Box

(Based on 'Magic Box' by Kit Wright)

I will put in my box . . .
The teeth of a vampire,
Dripping bright red blood.
The scythe of the Grim Reaper,
Silently choosing and killing its victims.

I will put in my box . . .
A witch's evil cackle,
As she flies swiftly through the air
On her black broomstick.
The face of a hideous gorgon,
Turning all who look at her into stone.

I will put in my box . . .
The eye of a tall Cyclops,
As it searches around greedily for its prey.
The low moan of a hungry zombie,
As it slowly rises out of its deep grave.

I will put in my box . . .
The long howl of an angry werewolf,
As it slowly stalks an unsuspecting soul.
The strength of an ugly ogre,
As it slowly raises its massive wooden club.

My box is made of
The bones of a skeleton,
As it drags its body along the floor.
The strength of a hulking troll,
As it swings its fist to crush its enemies.

My box is made of
Tough dragon hide,
That will keep unwanted visitors from stealing it.

Olly Smith (11)
Beachborough School

My Candy Box

(Based on 'Magic Box' by Kit Wright)

I will put in my box . . .
The first candy cane made
Representing Jesus' short life
And the lemon heads my father loves
With the smooth neon-yellow shell.

I will put in my box . . .
The blast of fruit gushers
As you take the first bite
And Haribo's newly made gummy bears
That you attempt to suck to the end.

I will put in my box . . .
The rattly sound of Skittles hitting the table
The sweet smell of fruits that taste really yummy
And the giant bubble of a Bazooka gum
With a big, big pop!

My box is made of
Old wrappers of loved sweet candy
And chips off the first store door
Held together with molten chocolate
And sewn with Haribo pasta.

Natalie Pack (11)
Beachborough School

Autumn Poem

A utumn conkers in their spiky cases
U nusual hedgehogs rustling in crunchy leaves
T rees with dead leaves falling
U nfathomable dark nights
M ice scurrying in hedgerows
N uts collected by careful squirrels

F ascinating spiders weaving lacy webs
U nerring birds begin migration
N umb Jack Frost fingers.

George Baker (10)
Beachborough School

Bonfire

There is a flaming, rampaging phoenix in my garden
Flying and surging
Showing his flaming wings
Above my trees
Where the leaves are falling silently
As the moon shines down.

I can see the fire burning off its wings
Flickering and then disappearing
In the black, cool, breezy sky
And now and again
If I look carefully
I can see it straight in the eye.

Flapping and pecking
At the cardboard and wood
And swallows it till
Hungry longer he is not
Suddenly his fire goes
And only a black crow is lying under the tree.

Ollie Breslin (10)
Beachborough School

Snow

The trees are covered in that beautiful snow,
Crystally, icy snow.
All at night when we're fast asleep
The wondrous snow, all cold and sleek
Whispers, 'Winter is here, winter is here,'
As the snowflakes form as one
In a blanket of untouched snow,
And as morning comes,
I look out of my window,
At that white, white wintry world,
Made from beautiful snow.

Olivia Treadwell (10)
Beachborough School

My Artist Box

(Based on 'Magic Box' by Kit Wright)

I will put in my box . . .
My first ever paintbox
And my first tentative painting
The talent inherited from my aunt
And a memory of an art museum visit.

I will put in my box . . .
A gold petal from Van Gogh's beautiful sunflowers,
A leaping ballet dancer from Renoir's palette,
The secret of Monet's flower garden
And a swish of an impressionist's paintbrush.

I will put in my box . . .
Picasso's feelings from terrible Guernica invoking great sorrow
Seurat's perfect pointillism dotting into infinity.

My box is made of
Ancient canvasses
Perfectly preserved
And bound with hog's hair,
It is locked for all time
Unless you have a passion for creativity.

Lucy Oram (11)
Beachborough School

Polar Bear Kennings

White coat wearer
Fish eater
Ice skater
Snow roller
Seal scarer
Slow runner
Sharp scratcher
Cub carer
Good camouflager
Fast swimmer.

Brad Wilfong (10)
Beachborough School

Winter Wonderland

W inter is white
 I ce is cold and slippery
N ice chocolate pudding makes my tummy warm
T reacle tarts are my favourite in winter
E armuffs keep me warm
R obins are stealing bread from the bird table.

W ater is all ice in winter
O n the pond people are playing
N aughty children throwing snowballs
D ark is lovely with trees all white
E veryone is outside playing in the snow
R abbits are in the hedge keeping warm
L andscapes like a huge fluffy blanket
A pple trees are sleeping under snow
N ervous mothers are watching children skating
D ark birds like dots are flying in the cold air.

Ellie Clark (9)
Beachborough School

Wicked Winter

W icked Jack Frost freezing everything in sight
 I cicles hanging from houses
C lothes covered in white snow
K nitted hats over our ears
E normous snowmen stand in fields
D ucks slipping on their frozen ponds.

W arming hot chocolate
 I n the house snoozing by the fire
N uts left out for the cold birds
T obogganing down slippery slopes
E veryone joining in the snowball fight
R obins floating in the air.

Harry Rymer (10)
Beachborough School

Winter Wonderland

W hite snow falling in the garden
I nterested birds left to freeze
N aughty schoolboys throwing snowballs
T errible snow storms block the road
E veryone is happy
R oaring fire in the living room.

W arm clothes ready to put on
O val-shaped snowmen glistening in the sun
N ight owls watch for prey
D arkness brings strange new stars
E veryone is out ice skating on the frozen pond
R oaring down the hill on your toboggan
L ovely mince pies and turkey for dinner
A mazing icicles glitter like jewelled necklaces
N ice hot chocolate to drink
D eer hunched up in the fields.

Toby Clark (10)
Beachborough School

White Winter

W hirling and whipping snow falls in the evening air
H eat yourself up by the fire
I ce skating in the park is fun
T obogganing down deep steep hills too
E ager children rush to build a snowman

W ebs like crystal hang from trees
I ce glistens on car windows
N ew stories are told to friends
T he crunch of snow as we walk on the path
E njoying hot chocolate on cold days
R inging wind chimes dangle in the air.

Garrett Hanson (9)
Beachborough School

Chess Box

(Based on 'Magic Box' by Kit Wright)

I would put in my box . . .
The first chessboard from when it all began,
With sparkling black and white squares.
The opening move of a chess champion
Playing for his next gold medal

I would put in my box . . .
The sound of a piece hitting the board
As the player checks the opposition,
The king trying to get out of check
From the magical queen and the marvellous castle

I would put in my box . . .
Becoming a champion
And being famous
All the moves to remember them always,
And the 64 squares

My box is made of
Shining golden wood
Like all the chess pieces
And is covered in black and white chess squares
It is locked with the cheer of the winning move.

James Chamberlain (10)
Beachborough School

Autumn Poem

A wesome Hallowe'en costumes frightening in the darkness
U nusual spiky conkers fall on your head like dropping bombs
T rees with beautiful multicoloured leaves
U nbearable weather and strong winds
M elons, apples, oranges are good to eat
N aughty squirrels stealing nuts and berries for storing

F ireworks boom in the sparkling night sky
U rgent animals running for shelter in tall trees
N utritious food, lovely for all to eat.

Harrison Coleman (11)
Beachborough School

Bonfire

There's an angry grey mare in my garden
Rearing and galloping
Snorting and glaring
Where the ground has come hard and cracked
From last year's sun

I can see her gleam from the sun
Gleaming and shining
Into the hot-red sky
And now again
If I watch I see a sad look in her eyes
In the mare's grey eyes.

Kicking and bucking her legs
For she's rearing and shying and bucking
Until she is tired
Then she fades away
Gone until next year.

Flora Scott (11)
Beachborough School

Wicked Winter

W et hats dripping from the snowball fight
 I n the snow a polar bear is searching for fish
C autious cats creeping carefully
K ites floating in freezing air
E nergetic schoolboys sliding on ice
D ucks puzzled by the frozen pond.

W ebs shining like jewels in the winter snow
 I n the hollow tree a baby hedgehog snores gently
N aughty children make snow angels
T rees stand like giant snowmen
E xcited dogs bark at melting snowflakes
R obins hop happily on crunchy snow.

Sandy Thompson (10)
Beachborough School

Bonfire

There is a fiery blue dragon in my garden
Running and snarling
He is flapping his wings
Sharp and pointed
Up in the sky
With the snow coming down

I can see his eyes through the window
Glinting and moving
Into the winter sky
And now and again
If I watch I can see
Water in his eyes

Snapping and swooping he tears
Old boxes and paper
And swallows them till
He is hungry no longer
But sleeps in a flutter of ashes
His wings lay still.

George Gardner (11)
Beachborough School

Piranha Kennings

Sea creature
Flesh eater
Teeth sharpener
Skeleton leaver
Spooky swimmer
Deadly biter
Fear bringer
River dweller
Furious glarer
Swift destroyer
Scary glower
Deep diver
Orange cover.

Thomas Gordon-Colebrooke (10)
Beachborough School

Bonfire

There is a big crocodile in my garden
Snapping and crunching,
Slashing his scaly tail
Behind the thorn bushes
Where red berries glisten
Under the moonlit sky.

I can see his fierce eyes
Staring and blinking
In the long grass
And now and again
I see his spiky back rippling under the leaves.

Snapping and grabbing
He chops
All the dead leaves and old wood
And gulps them down.
Hungry no longer
He sleeps again
With one eye open.

Jacob Stilp (10)
Beachborough School

Dragon Kennings

Fire breather
Deadly killer
Scaly winger
Human eater
Wild hunter
Cave wanderer
Meat eater
Sky ruler
Treasure guarder
Cloud flier
Tail swisher
Knight slayer.

Calum Miller (10)
Beachborough School

My Mythical Creatures Box

(Based on 'Magic Box' by Kit Wright)

I will put in my box . . .
The angry roar of the Minotaur, as he prowls his spooky labyrinth,
The poisonous fang of the Hydra, as it clamps onto its prey,
The terrifying neigh of the man-eating horses,
as they demand their food
And the mesmerising swing of the snakes on Medusa's head.

I will put in my box . . .
The hissing flame of the dragon, guarding its lair,
The hulking mass of the Titan, as it stomps towards its prey,
The perilous song of the sirens, luring sailors to watery graves
And the dangerous peck of the Griffin, trying to pierce its victim.

I will put in my box . . .
The three heads of Cerberus, as he guards the gate to Hades,
A prickle from a Manticore's back, which rustles in the wind,
The groping tentacles of the Cracken,
as it brings down an unfortunate ship
And the crackling of the phoenix
as it rises from the smouldering ashes.

My box is made of
The scaly skin of a dragon
And the Minotaur's horn padlock,
With a Hydra fang key.

Joshua Lauder (11)
Beachborough School

Bonfire

There's a big poisonous adder in my garden
Slithering and searching
Showing me his big poisonous teeth
Beside my bedroom window
Where the darkness creeps
Silently through the night

I can see his big forked tongue
Flashing and flicking
Down in the long grass
And now and again
If I watch I can see him
Showing me a tiny eye

Glinting and plunging
He rips old things left over
And gobbles them
Till he is too tired to gobble anymore
He sleeps under all the ash
His sharp forked tongue curled up in his mouth.

Jasper Church (11)
Beachborough School

White Winter

W inter is wonderful
H ard ice is on the frozen lake
I ce sculptures melt in the winter sun
T all trees cast dark shadows
E everyone enjoying frothy hot chocolate

W ebs like crystals shine
I ndoors the fire crackles
N aughty children are eating snowflakes
T ired hedgehogs curl up in hollow trees
E xcited boys skate on the frozen pond
R estless snow falls on shining rooftops,
   we sledge down steep slopes.

Alyssa Purvis (9)
Beachborough School

Bonfire

There is a fierce golden stallion in my garden,
Biting and prancing,
Showing his great power
Around the pond
Where the ground is crinkled and hard
With cracked bricks.

I can see his tail by the trees
Swishing and shining
In the calm, cool night.
Here and there
When I watch him he prances,
A powerful king.

Glinting and punching he rips,
Old bills and toys
And chews them till
He can go no longer,
But falls safely,
Then quickly fades away.

Emily Dove (11)
Beachborough School

Winter Wonder

W onderful webs glistening like crystals
 I nternational skiing stadiums
N aughty children hiding in snowy places
T oddlers putting on snow suits
E veryone is excited
R ecklessly skating on ice.

W intry snowflakes falling on children's tongues
O thers stay and play 'put the nose on the reindeer'
N aughty squirrels fighting over acorns
D ogs dressed in Christmas clothes
E ager children want to go outside
R eally huge snowmen stand like soldiers.

Darius Robinson (10)
Beachborough School

Bonfire

There's a competitive racehorse in my garden,
Rearing and shying,
Nervously neighing,
Under the red tender fire of the trees,
With smoking ash firing out,
In the glistening midnight moon.

I can see her breath,
Floating around the burnings
Of the remaining life
Underneath the anger,
And now and again you see
A drop of water,
Burning, it's coming and going,
Once every autumn.

Dropping a tear
Of a burning life
And burning fear,
Infinitely stops,
Crying as it lays down,
To a disappointment of her hoofs.

Ella Markham (10)
Beachborough School

My Pony Box

(Based on 'Magic Box' by Kit Wright)

I will put in my box . . .
The hungry munching of my plump pony,
The musky smell of his coat
And the gruesome sight of his teeth.

I will put in my box . . .
The heart-thudding pound of hooves
As he races towards his hay,
The soft feel of his velvety nose,
As he pokes his head over the stable door.

I will put in my box . . .
The incredible feeling as we bounce
In a rising canter,
And the soaring thrill of our first jump.

My box is made of
The softest saddle leather,
It is lined with a woollen blanket,
Securing its edges are metal whips
And it is locked with lucky horseshoes.

Eve Von Der Heyde (10)
Beachborough School

Space Flight

Rockets flying everywhere
Seeing aliens is very rare
Everybody running round
Or flying at the speed of sound!

Aliens hiding in their holes
Or sucking out the human souls
Burning bodies in the night
You wouldn't want to see that sight!

Simon Walker (10)
Blakesley CE Primary School

Space Dance

Stars, galaxies, planets and moons.
Why am I dancing with aliens with spoons?
They call me God of the Dancing Star
But I don't have a clue of which species they are.
They go *ploop-ploop*, but which language do they talk?
All I do is smile and moonwalk.
We do a big dance and we do a little chant.
The king comes out - looking like my great aunt!
He smiled at me and then said,
'All of the ploop-ploops go to bed!'

Bradley Harper (11)
Blakesley CE Primary School

Space

Shooting stars sparkling bright
In the middle of the night.
Rockets flying through the air
Moonlight glistening everywhere.

Planets floating near and far
Aliens driving their brand new space car
Aliens popping out their heads
From their little alien eggs.

Harry Rolph (10)
Blakesley CE Primary School

Space Message

I'm on the moon, in space,
Having fun with moon dust,
Looking at the stars!

Wondering about different planets,
Saturn, Jupiter and Mars,
Orbiting the sun with comets in-between.
Studying the stars now,
I don't want to go home!

Laura Pratley (10)
Blakesley CE Primary School

Aliens

Aliens on the planet Mars
Getting fat on chocolate bars.
Astronauts floating by.
Aliens thinking, I could make astronaut pie.

Me and my team on a mission
But I'm having trouble with the ignition.
All of the eyes looking at an orbit
All of the aliens are called Norbert.

Jak Wilson (9)
Blakesley CE Primary School

Space Mission

I'm in my rocket flying through space,
Looking for an alien.
I'm flying from planet to planet
And I end up on the moon.
I'm looking around
And what do I see?
An alien has found me!
I take it home to show everybody.

Katie Noble (10)
Blakesley CE Primary School

Space

In space there are lots of wondrous planets.
On those wondrous planets are deep craters.
In those craters live diminutive, wiry, musty aliens.
Inside those aliens are lots of love and care.
Outside those aliens are deep craters.
Outside those deep craters are lots of other planets.
Outside those planets are lots of sparkly constellations
and clusters of stars.

Shannon Parker (11)
Blakesley CE Primary School

Tornado Hit Bozeat

Swirling wind ripped trees to pieces,
The violent rotating whirlwind caused people hurt,
Pieces of houses flying over my head,
A dangerous, deadly, powerful mini torpedo,
The school had its chairs and tables flying everywhere,
Then the twister struck the power station and all the lights went off,
Suddenly another tornado appeared and then another,
The tornadoes caused destruction,
Houses have been spun away and many lives were lost,
Bozeat is a total mess from the two tornadoes.

Oliver Millin (9)
Bozeat Primary School

Football Crazy

I'm a . . .
hot shooting
sliding, tackling
quick tripping
goal scoring
happy landing
break dancing
somersaulting
crowd saluting
pistol packing
rockin', rollin'
diving, sliding
head breaking
quick shooting
back flippin'
rolly polly
cracking feet
rootin'-tootin'
fast runner
fast dodging
booting far.

Tom Lamb (10)
Bozeat Primary School

The Eagle

He flies in the misty sky,
Twirls round, rocks as he goes by,
His feathers are a pearly white,
He is enjoying this midnight flight,
His beak is yellow with a pointed end,
The body of this bird is able to bend,
He lands on a seashell wall,
Making sure he does not fall.

Lauren Betts (10)
Bozeat Primary School

Car

A car is an . . .
ozone wreckin'
tyre burnin'
wheel spinnin'
road wreckin'
Money eatin'
Petrol drinkin'
Loud soundin'
Sweet lookin'
Speed ticket gettin'
Police chasin'
Fast lookin'
Money winnin'
Spoiler havin'
Engine growlin'
Mean machine.

Jamie Field (10)
Bozeat Primary School

Beauty

It is the colour of light blue,
It smells like sweet, sweet roses,
It looks like a sunflower growing in the sun,
It feels like the warm summer sun.

Tilly Finch (8)
Bozeat Primary School

The Sea

The sea is a wild cat
Huge and black
He prowls on the beach all day
With lashing claws and fierce teeth
Hour upon hour he roars
The rolling pebbles washing on the beach,
And he runs, runs, runs!
The huge sea cat kicks,
All the stones.

And when the night breeze cries
And the sun hides in a distant land
He jumps on his feet and howls and howls,
Shaking his wet feet around the edge of the cliffs,
And prowls and shouts long and loud.

But on warm days in June or July,
Whenever the sand's on the beach
Play no more the grassy tune,
He rolls on the pebbly shores,
So quiet,
So silent,
He quietly sleeps.

Alex Harrison (11)
Bozeat Primary School

The Horrorjon

If you take a stroll by the River Bon,
You'd better look out for the Horrorjon.
It has a brown head as rough as pines,
On little boys and girls it dines.
Its teeth are as sharp as knives,
If you see it, run for your lives.
It has a huge green tail,
It will hit you without fail.
And if those teeth close around you,
He'll crunch and munch you, that's what he'll do.

Thomas Houghton (11)
Bozeat Primary School

The Sea

The sea is millions of angry horses
galloping down the shore.
The sea is puppies
biting at your feet and shoes.
The sea is eagles
stalking their prey.
The sea is white mice
running from their enemies.
The sea is kittens
biting and playing.
The sea is tigers
praying for shade.
The sea is children
playing and working.
Those are the seas,
the seven seas.

Eleanor Downes (10)
Bozeat Primary School

Tiger, Tiger

Tiger, tiger, what a beast!
In the night a deer for a feast.

Tiger, tiger on the roll,
The king cat could kill a troll.
A deadly hunter in the night
Meet up with the beast,
You will have a fright!

Tiger, tiger, burning bright,
Your stripes give me a big fat fright.
Orange and black in your pack -
When you run your stripes are a blur,
When you lay on the forest floor you purr!

Alannah Gray (10)
Bozeat Primary School

The Commentator

This is your commentator
live from the High Street.
It is a fine day to play football.
Oh dear, it looks like Sam has fallen over
by doing a slide tackle.
Oh look, Sam has got back up.
It's Sam to Owen,
Owen back to Sam,
oh is it a goal?
Oh no, it's not!
Oh no, Sam has been tackled by the other team,
here comes Sam, speeding to try and get the ball.
What an excellent slide tackle from Sam,
oh no, where's the ball gone?
It's gone over to Mrs Spence's.
Sam has got on his bike
and he opens the gate,
what's he doing?
Mrs Spence and Mr Spence are asleep outside,
he's fabulous,
he passes Mrs Spence and Mr Spence,
he gets the ball.
Sam now runs to the gate . . .

Bethanie Bonnar (10)
Bozeat Primary School

The Eagle

He swoops up and down in the midnight sky,
Side to side he will fly,
His feathers are a metallic grey,
On the rocks he will stay,
The moon shines onto the dark sea,
Trying to catch his fish for tea,
He swiftly flies down to the golden sand,
On the shore he will stand.

Molly Betts (11)
Bozeat Primary School

A Football Poem

I'm a heart breakin'
goal makin'
back flippin'
ball dippin'
goal scorin'
never borin'
slide tacklin'
ankles crackin'
crowd lovin'
always shovin'
hot shootin'
always bootin'
autograph signin'
never winnin'
Rooney's enemy
and Craig Bellamy.

Oliver Bartell (9)
Bozeat Primary School

Thunder And Lightning

The lightning hit a house,
It flattened a mouse,
The thunder was like a lion, roaring
It scared the woodlouse,
The lightning flashed,
As the thunder crashed,
It boomed like stamping
And like elephants trampling,
Thunder and lightning
Is very, very frightening.

Laurence Edmunds (9)
Bozeat Primary School

The Door

(Based on 'The Door' by Miroslav Holub)

Go and open the door
maybe there's a funfair with a golden wheel
maybe there's an old dusty castle on the tip of a green hill
maybe there's a building site full of men working hard.

Go and open the door
maybe there's a bowling alley
with many people in there having fun
or a small town with many kind villagers
in the colourful market.

Go and open the door
maybe there's a hard-working school
with clever children being taught
or a new planet with green aliens waddling around
or maybe you'll find me!

James Dylag (8)
Hall Meadow Primary School

Go And Open The Door

(Based on 'The Door' by Miroslav Holub)

Go and open the door
maybe there will be
a magnificent, magical waterfall
shimmering like sapphires in the moonlight.

Go and open the door
maybe there's a magical world
that whenever you touch a Christmas tree decoration
it turns into a cup of hot chocolate, oozing in the sun.

Go and open the door
there could probably be
a warm and cosy home for me,
or maybe none of these things I expect,
but my own small beloved family.

Nadiya Rahumtulla (9)
Hall Meadow Primary School

The Door

(Based on 'The Door' by Miroslav Holub)

Go and open the door
maybe there's a spotty monster
combing his fur.

Go and open the door
maybe there's a pink panther
lazing in a tree.

Go and open the door
maybe there's a fairy
fluttering in a tree.

Go and open the door
maybe there's a fat man
relaxing in a jacuzzi.

Go and open the door
maybe there's a multicoloured dog
chasing a fat cat.

Lexie Grzywna (9)
Hall Meadow Primary School

The Door

(Based on 'The Door' by Miroslav Holub)

Go and open the door
maybe there's a chocolate pony
galloping round the fresh green field
or an oozing cocoa river floating round and round.

Go and open the door
maybe there's a jazzy bowling alley
or a kitten playing with a pink stripy ball.

Go and open the door
maybe there's a forest with leaves floating.

Georgia Goodwin (9)
Hall Meadow Primary School

The Door

(Based on 'The Door' by Miroslav Holub)

Go and open the door
maybe there's a dark, freezing cave with bats
or a magic sword with shiny glitter.

Go and open the door
maybe there's a gold unicorn running
or a chocolate coloured dog walking.

Go and open the door
maybe there's a dark, wet, stinking wood
with lots of scary animals
or maybe a giant with ripped clothes.

Go and open the door
maybe there's a forest
with green leaves and crunchy branches
with cracking trees.

Go and open the door
maybe there's a wicked wizard.

Dylan Birk (9)
Hall Meadow Primary School

The Door

(Based on 'The Door' by Miroslav Holub)

Go and open the door
maybe there's a dark forbidden alley
with eyeless red beasts
scaling their way up.

Go and open the door
maybe there's a sky
with dotted pink and blue stars here and there
and people making a wish.

Grace Pearson (8)
Hall Meadow Primary School

Go And Open The Door

(Based on 'The Door' by Miroslav Holub)

Go and open the door
Maybe there's a murky sewer,
With a distinctive smell.

Maybe there's an untamed snake,
Preparing to strike
Or a never-ending hole,
Going down through the centre of the Earth.

Go and open the door
Maybe there's a grumpy old lady,
Her handbag at the ready,
Or another door,
With a silvery gold handle
And an identical door behind it.

Go and open the door
Maybe you will just find me!

Christopher Lane (9)
Hall Meadow Primary School

Go And Open The Door

(Based on 'The Door' by Miroslav Holub)

Go and open the door
Maybe there's a big bird
Flying past the chocolate mountains.

Go and open the door
Maybe there's a star
Soaring past the clouds.

Go and open the door
Maybe there's nothing.

Javan Bajwa (8)
Hall Meadow Primary School

Go And Open The Door

(Based on 'The Door' by Miroslav Holub)

Go and open the door
Maybe there's a chilly ice cube,
Sprinkled with lemon juice and sugar.

Go and open the door
Maybe there's a wacky wardrobe
With brown clashing doors.

Go and open the door
Maybe there's a gold palm tree
Stuffed with rosemary and spices
Or maybe there's the sound of screams
Echoing across the corridor.

Go and open the door
Maybe there's a face, very pale
Covered with streaming blood
But you'll see a swishing, curly chocolate mousse delight.

Molly Eyles
Hall Meadow Primary School

Go And Open The Door

(Based on 'The Door' by Miroslav Holub)

Go and open the door,
Maybe there's a fearsome tiger
With teeth like blades of knives,
Or a shimmering white unicorn
That has magic floating around it.

Go and open the door,
Maybe there's a humongous, vicious mouse,
Or a terrifying scaly dragon waiting for his tea.

Go and open the door,
Maybe there's a tremendous talking fish,
Swishing its tail here and there,
Or maybe there's nothing
Except a tiny bag of wishes waiting to be made.

Emily Lear (9)
Hall Meadow Primary School

The Door
(Based on 'The Door' by Miroslav Holub)

Go and open the door
Maybe there's a dark dog chasing its tail,
A football stadium with fans cheering for 90 minutes,
Or a medieval fort shooting down enemies.

Go and open the door
Maybe there's a chocolate river with Cadbury 99s swimming about,
A treasure chest with golden coins filled inside
Or a water fountain with a three-eyed fish floating about.

Go and open the door
Maybe there's a school teaching people,
A venus flytrap catching all the insects
Or a dirty river with people dying beside it.

Danny Rashley (9)
Hall Meadow Primary School

Go And Open The Door
(Based on 'The Door' by Miroslav Holub)

Go and open the door
Maybe there's some luscious green grass
To tickle your taste buds.
Maybe there's oozing, melting chocolate
Dribbling down the next-door neighbour's mouth.

Go and open the door
Maybe there's a cute purple poodle
Panting for food.
Maybe there's a shining glitter ball
You can see from miles away.

Go and open the door
You may just find me.

Sophie Ellidge (8)
Hall Meadow Primary School

The Door

(Based on 'The Door' by Miroslav Holub)

Go and open the door
Maybe there's a fairy with golden wings,
A pink poodle with blue eyes
Or a chocolate mountain with sugar flowers.

Go and open the door
Maybe there's a silvery moon glinting in the night,
A lavender garden
Or a blossom bush.

Go and open the door
Maybe there's a newborn baby,
A green meadow
Or a gold and silver sunset.

Go and open the door
Maybe there's nothing,
Just my own loving family.

Chloe Linnell (9)
Hall Meadow Primary School

The Door

(Based on 'The Door' by Miroslav Holub)

Go and open the door
Maybe, there's a lovely sparkling chocolate ink cartridge,
Or a wood, with golden treasure, which I'll find.

Go and open the door
Maybe, there's a flying, gliding red car
Or a plastic bottle, flying in the distance.

Go and open the door,
Maybe, there's nothing.

Luke Doughty (9)
Hall Meadow Primary School

Go And Open The Door

(Based on 'The Door' by Miroslav Holub)

Go and open the door
maybe there's a . . .
flying dog up high
in the pink blossom clouds
or a golden unicorn
drinking from riverbanks,
or a wonderful factory
making all of the chocolate fountains.

Go and open the door
maybe there's a . . .
multicoloured rock
lazing beside the deep blue sea,
or a pink bird flying
over the chimney tops,
or maybe there's nothing.

Courtney Ashley (8)
Hall Meadow Primary School

The Door

(Based on 'The Door' by Miroslav Holub)

Go and open the door
Maybe there's . . .
A magical city
And the only colour is blue.

Go and open the door
Maybe there's . . .
A monster land where there's only monsters
And nothing else.

Georgina Gallagher (9)
Hall Meadow Primary School

Go And Open The Door

(Based on 'The Door' by Miroslav Holub)

Go and open the door
maybe there's a joyful music land
with floating notes filling the air,
or a dreamy white Pegasus
soaring through the purple sunset,
or a pink fairy fluttering gracefully.

Go and open the door
maybe there's twinkling shells
glinting like stars
or a cute kitten
playing with a ball of wool.

Go and open the door
maybe there's the sparkling stars
rising into the midnight sky,
or maybe there's just me.

Sophie Simmonds (9)
Hall Meadow Primary School

Go And Open The Door

(Based on 'The Door' by Miroslav Holub)

Go and open the door
maybe there's a splashing river with chocolate fish,
a wild hot jungle
or a magical world with fairies in.

Go and open the door
maybe there's a rabbit hutch with cute rabbits in,
a waterfall with glitter hanging down
or wild lavender with petals drooping.

Go and open the door
maybe there's a dead bird with feathers on the ground
or a graceful shimmering white mountain.

Alicia Silcock (8)
Hall Meadow Primary School

Go And Open The Door

(Based on 'The Door' by Miroslav Holub)

Go and open the door
maybe there's a blue, beautiful butterfly
with pink and silver stripes on its wings.

Go and open the door
maybe there's the sweaty, hot, scorching savannah
with noisy rattling snakes.

Maybe there are some animals you like,
the nibbling hamster and the silent seal
and the shiny tortoise and the beautiful penguin
and the *magnificent* dolphin.

Go and open the door
maybe there's a murderer that has hands
filled with someone's blood
or a heart in the middle of an archer's target.

Jessica Hallett (8)
Hall Meadow Primary School

Go And Open The Door

(Based on 'The Door' by Miroslav Holub)

Go and open the door
Maybe there's an oozing chocolate factory
That smells like exploding sweets
Or a dark, horrible haunted house
With screams every second.

Go and open the door
Maybe there's a freezing cold ice castle
With people marching everywhere!

James Garratt (8)
Hall Meadow Primary School

Go And Open The Door

(Based on 'The Door' by Miroslav Holub)

Go and open the door
maybe there's dribbling chocolate running down a lake,
with a sprinkle of milk buttons on top.

Maybe a planet covered with polka-dot ribbons
full of aliens plodding their way round.

Go and open the door
maybe there's a giant bear
screaming his head off,
smells like a skunk wagging his tail
or maybe a dolphin leaping and bouncing over the sea.

Go and open the door
maybe there's my grandpa
snoozing away in his armchair.

Leah Milligan (8)
Hall Meadow Primary School

Go And Open The Door

(Based on 'The Door' by Miroslav Holub)

Go and open the door
maybe there's a golden unicorn
riding on a dark blue magic carpet.

Go and open the door
maybe there's a vampire eating a bread wall
or a waterfall shimmering ice cream on the bread.

Go and open the door
maybe there's a pony trotting in the dark green, graceful grass
or a monster gobbling a house.

Amy McHarg (9)
Hall Meadow Primary School

Go And Open The Door

(Based on 'The Door' by Miroslav Holub)

Go and open the door
Maybe there's . . .
A gentle cream-coloured pony trotting,
Dreamily round the soft, green grass
Or maybe there's a lilac puppy
Playing with a squeaky pink ball.

Go and open the door
Maybe there's . . .
A purple, dreamy fairy
Fluttering softly to one green lily pad
To another over the clear bubbly stream.

Go and open the door
Maybe there's . . .
A tropical mermaid
Diving in and out the salty sea,
With a blue friendly dolphin following beside her.

Grace Read (8)
Hall Meadow Primary School

Go And Open The Door

(Based on 'The Door' by Miroslav Holub)

Go and open the door
maybe there's a striped and sunny football pitch ready for winners
or the A14 bringing traffic or a busy, noisy airport stuffed with Ryanairs,
an old man slurping his tea.

Go and open the door
maybe there's a brown cardboard box waiting for me
or just nothing sitting there on a wooden bench,
a hippo paddling in its manure pile!

Go and open the door . . .

Sebastian Winstone (9)
Hall Meadow Primary School

Go And Open The Door

(Based on 'The Door' by Miroslav Holub)

Go and open the door
Maybe there's the freezing cold Arctic,
Full of life.

Go and open the door
Maybe there's an oozy thick chocolate world
With a long tube.

Go and open the door
Maybe there's a shimmering magic unicorn
Gliding over the moon.

Go and open the door
Maybe there's a massive, spiky scorpion
Gobbling human flesh.

Emily Singh (9)
Hall Meadow Primary School

The Door

(Based on 'The Door' by Miroslav Holub)

Go and open the door,
maybe there's a huge monster
stamping up a hill
or a humongous ant stealing stuff.

Maybe there's a beautiful beach
with waving flags or a river
slowly going past.

Maybe there's yucky mud
hanging from a tree.

Oliver McIvor (8)
Hall Meadow Primary School

The Door

(Based on 'The Door' by Miroslav Holub)

Go and open the door
maybe there's a . . .
pink puppy chasing its tail
or a purple unicorn galloping in a field.

Go and open the door
maybe there's a . . .
silver-winged fairy dozing in a buttercup,
or a goldfish swirling in its fish bowl.

Go and open the door
maybe there's a . . .
white tiger roaring on a hard rock
or a runny dripping chocolate fountain.

Go and open the door
maybe there's a . . .
cinema full of films
or a dolphin splashing its tail.

Go and open the door
maybe there's a world full of life
or maybe there's just *me!*

Holly Foster (9)
Hall Meadow Primary School

Go And Open The Door

(Based on 'The Door' by Miroslav Holub)

Go and open the door
Maybe there's a perfect purple puppy tracking its bone
Or even a dumb dolphin dancing in the deep blue sea.

Go and open the door
Maybe there's a cute cat scratching away at a piece of wood
Or even a factory with melting chocolate.

Go and open the door
Maybe there's a garden full of green grass
Or even a hamster nibbling on a piece of brown crunchy food.

Go and open the door
Maybe there's a huge lump of crunchy fluffy sky all on its own
Or even a cloud that is fluffy and soft.

Go and open the door
Maybe there's a floating bed that's comfy and warm
Or even a school with teachers teaching.

Go and open the door
Maybe there's a bluebird singing away
Or even a boy with scuffy hair walking to school.

Abbie Strowbridge-Knight (8)
Hall Meadow Primary School

Fun

Fun is yellow like fresh spring flowers.
Fun is like laughter all around.
Fun tastes like chocolate yoghurt dripping off my spoon.
Fun smells like candyfloss, fluffy and pink.
Fun looks like playing football on the green grass in the park.
Fun feels like 'please, let me do it again'.
Fun reminds me of me and my friends.

Ryan Waller (9)
Long Buckby Junior School

Aliens Invade London!

Aliens are invading London,
They encroach upon every construction,
They're burglarising all the shops
And abducting all the flabbergasted cops.

Some slimy serpents slither,
While slime spits silver splodges onto silent state tribes,
Meanwhile, more mad monsters munch muesli in the morning,
While mortified multitudes melt into mud.

Their polished transporter gleams under the sun like a golden angel,
Windows blind passers-by with dazzlement,
Scents of ancient tea, wafts through rough cracks,
Satellite aerials tower above the complicated machine.

These pongy, stinky, ruthless, cheeky, terrible-mannered,
Nosy and sneaky, do-not-speak-our-language monsters
Have to stop!
So . . . *bang!* . . . and the aliens pop!

Theanora Criswell-Sanderson (10)
Long Buckby Junior School

Hate

Hate is black like tarmac.
Hate sounds like nails screeching down a blackboard.
Hate is sour.
Hate has the stench of rotten eggs.
Hate looks like food being munched up in someone's mouth.
Hate feels like someone standing on your chest.
Hate is the worst feeling you can get.

Oliver Ball (9)
Long Buckby Junior School

Stars

Shining stars
Big and small
Looking round the world,
Every night
Nice and light.

Yellows and gold
Shining down
On houses and villages,
Every night
Nice and light.

Hundreds and thousands
Doing what
Every star should do,
Every night
Nice and light.

Callum Evans (9)
Long Buckby Junior School

Love

Love is like bright red poppies in green fields.
Love is the sound of singing birds in the spring.
Love tastes of delicious cakes, chocolate and all things sweet.
Love smells of gorgeous roses in the garden in the summertime.
Love is my family when we're all getting along.
Love feels warm like a burning red-hot fire.
Love reminds me of hearts, happiness and hugs.

Poppy Roberts (9)
Long Buckby Junior School

Silence

Silence is golden
Silence is hush
Silence is heard
When you fermer la bouche
('Close the mouth' in French).

Silence is quiet
As quiet as a mouse
Silence is nobody
Inside a house.

Silence is boring
I prefer noise
The sound of me
Playing with all my toys.

Silence is for adults
It's not for a child
So make a lot of noise
And drive Mum and Dad wild.

Jamie Goodridge (9)
Long Buckby Junior School

Investigation - Haikus

Creaky cup cracking,
Bubblewrap popping loudly,
Shiny foil rough now.

Ten minutes gone now,
Temperature going down,
Sixty minutes gone.

Ridwan Choudhury (9)
Oakway Junior School

Dropping And Rising Temperature - Haikus

Comfort, fluffy, smooth,
Cracking, popping cups, make an
Investigation?

Rising temperature,
Ten minute wait, watching the
Thermometer . . . *pop!*

Now I know what is
An insulator and a
Conductor, crackle.

Janki Gokani (9)
Oakway Junior School

The Frozen Hand - Haikus

Icy, smooth and cold
Rock solid, slippy and wet
So cold, don't touch it!

Wet and slippy, cool
The fingers are melting now
Sloppy and ice-cold.

Sharp fingers and wet
Puddling now and so sloppy
Oh no, it's melted!

Troy Franklin
Oakway Junior School

The Frozen Hand - Haikus

Freezing, icy hand,
Solid, slippy, white but cold!
Fingers smooth and wet.

See it melting fast!
Dripping, drooping but still cold
Puddle forming, wow!

Sloppy puddle, why?
Scary claws, pointy fingers
It is dissolved, why?

Natt Redden
Oakway Junior School

The Frozen Hand - Haikus

It's hard and frozen,
Solid fingers, cold and white,
Be careful, it's smooth!

Oh no, it's melting!
It's turning into liquid.
Why is it dripping?

Oh gosh, it's melted
A puddle underneath it.
It is now liquid.

Luke Nevett (9)
Oakway Junior School

Frozen Ice Hand - Haikus

Frozen ice lolly,
Cold and white, hard and see-through,
Look out, it is hard!

Dripping and melting,
It's turning into liquid,
Watch, it will wet you.

Melted to water,
Just a puddle from now on,
No ice lolly now.

Timmy Thompson (9)
Oakway Junior School

Frozen Hand - Haikus

It is frozen hard.
Why is it so cold as well?
It is solid wet.

Why is it dripping?
Because it is melting, wet
Puddle is coming.

Oh no, it's fading.
That the clearing has now gone.
Oh it's gone away.

Jack Rooney (9)
Oakway Junior School

The Frozen Hand - Haikus

It's a frozen hand!
See-through hand, smooth and wet ice,
Why is it solid?

It's got a puddle
It's turning into liquid
Is it warmer yet?

Look it's melting quick
It's got a massive puddle
No! It's liquid now!

Emma Humphries (9)
Oakway Junior School

The Ice Hand - Haikus

I found a cold hand,
I picked it up and shivered.
Watch out, it's freezing!

I went back to see,
Drip-drop, drip-drop, it's drooping.
Watch out, it's melting!

I went back again,
Oh no, please don't melt, not now!
Oh, it has melted!

Attina Brown (8)
Oakway Junior School

Frozen Hand - Haikus

Solid, rock and fat
It's really cold, hard and wet.
Why should you forget!

Less freezing, ice-cold,
Would you like to see it? *Wow!*
Melting now, oh no!

Really melting now,
Tell the teacher now! Oh no!
(Why has it melted?)

Sophie Burgess (8)
Oakway Junior School

Frozen Hand - Haikus

Slippery, wet ice,
Heavy, bubbly and ugly.
Freezing, solid, smooth.

Spiky, liquid, soft,
Slimy, melted, big fat hand.
Oh why did you melt?

Reshma Begum (9)
Oakway Junior School

My Haikus

Bubbly, crispy wrap
So cold, liquid in a cup
Some made a big pop.

Test the temperature
Make sure it is on the spot
It might be colder.

Will it go higher?
Maybe it will go lower
Let us find it out.

Nathan Carter (8)
Oakway Junior School

Frozen Hand - Haikus

Water is frozen,
Hand is slippery and cold.
Hand, icy and melts!

Melting now, oh no!
It's dripping, it's melting, no!
It's melting, it is!

It is a puddle!
Oh no, what is happening?
Oh, it's melted now.

Annabella Costantino (9)
Oakway Junior School

Beyond The Door

(Based on 'The Door' by Miroslav Holub)

Go and open the door.
Maybe there's a fairy
who flutters in the sky.
Maybe there's a shimmering moon
shining over a lost city.
Maybe there's a unicorn
who flies way up into the foggy clouds
or maybe there's a swimming pool
in the stars.

Go and open the door.
Maybe there's a sun
that shines brightly.
Maybe there's a treasure box
with a thousand pots of gold.
Maybe there's a hungry cat
that prowls the dusty city
or a magic carpet
that flies around the world.

Go and open the door.
Maybe there's a running dog
that barks for all the world to hear.
Maybe there's a yellow star
that's shining brightly in the sky.
Maybe there's a fish
that loves swimming in the dark sea
or maybe there's a fog
but it will soon clear
and there will be somewhere to go.

Emily Reed (7)
Pitsford Primary School

Beyond The Door

(Based on 'The Door' by Miroslav Holub)

Go and open the door.
Maybe there's a shining bright moon.
Maybe there's a unicorn
splashing in the waves
or a shimmering pool
sinking in the sky.

Go and open the door.
Maybe there's a hairy mammoth
with gigantic tusks.
Maybe there's a doctor
who's fighting his enemies
or maybe there's a dog
singing for its supper.

Go and open the door.
Maybe there's a forest
with lots and lots of animals.
Maybe there's a star
that's fallen from the sky
or maybe there's an elephant
spraying lots of water.

Go and open the door.
Maybe you'll see a face
or an eye watching you.

Joshua Jess (9)
Pitsford Primary School

Beyond The Door

(Based on 'The Door' by Miroslav Holub)

Go and open the door.
Maybe there's a glittering star
glowing in the sky.
Maybe there's a fairy fluttering its wings
in the deep, dark sky.
Maybe there's a golden sunset
on the ground
or a dog barking
or thick snow that you can walk in.

Go and open the door.
Maybe there's a rainbow
with all different colours.
Maybe there's a jungle
with animals making horrible sounds.
Maybe there's a treasure box
glittering with gold and silver.
Maybe there's a sailing boat
sailing through the wavy sea
or a unicorn with lovely wings.

Go and open the door.
At least there will be something there.

Lucy Richmond (7)
Pitsford Primary School

Beyond The Door

(Based on 'The Door' by Miroslav Holub)

Go and open the door.
Maybe there's a giant sparkling star
floating around
waiting for you.
Maybe there's a spotty unicorn
with pink wings
galloping around
in the snow
or maybe there's a rainbow
waiting for you to walk across it
and find the pot of gold.

Go and open the door.
Maybe there's a fairy
waiting to give you money
from the tooth that's gone.
Maybe there's a sleepy teddy
waiting to go to bed
or maybe there's a chocolate fountain
running through your fingers.

Go and open the door.
At least there will be
a gust of wind.

Chloe Cooper (8)
Pitsford Primary School

Beyond The Door

(Based on 'The Door' by Miroslav Holub)

Go and open the door.
Maybe there's a giant teddy bear
just waiting to give you a hug.
Maybe there's a pink limo with wings
desperate to swoop you away
to a far-off land
or maybe there's a fairy with a wand
ready to turn you into a beautiful princess.

Go and open the door.
Maybe there's an enchanted forest
creaking as the trees talk to each other.
Maybe there's a lonely clock ticking
as it reaches my bedtime.
Maybe there's a flaming fire
shooting for the stars.

Go and open the door.
At least there will be another side
to explore.

Meg Bamford (9)
Pitsford Primary School

Beyond The Door

(Based on 'The Door' by Miroslav Holub)

Go and open the door.
Maybe there's a long swimming pool
glittering in the sun.
Maybe there's a dark moon
in outer space.
Maybe there's a rainbow
in the sky
or maybe there's a friendly dog
barking very quietly.
Go and open the door.
At least there will be a sound.

Charlie Lloyd (7)
Pitsford Primary School

Beyond The Door

(Based on 'The Door' by Miroslav Holub)

Go and open the door.
Maybe there's a shining star
up in the bright sky.
Maybe there's a rainbow
down the hill
or maybe there's a lost city.

Go and open the door.
Maybe there's a bright moon
up in a big dark sky.
Maybe there's a shining sun
shimmering everywhere.
Maybe there's a dog running up and down
or maybe there's a fog
that will not clear.

Olivia Bott (8)
Pitsford Primary School

Beyond The Door

(Based on 'The Door' by Miroslav Holub)

Go and open the door.
Maybe there's a giant sea horse
floating on a milky coconut.
Maybe there's a flying fish
diving backwards
or maybe there's thirteen gnomes
dancing round a fire
or a golden castle
shimmering under the silky moon.

Go and open the door.
At least there will be
your footsteps.

Huw Redwood (8)
Pitsford Primary School

Beyond The Door

(Based on 'The Door' by Miroslav Holub)

Go and open the door.
Maybe there's a chocolate fountain
dripping hot melted chocolate to the floor.
Maybe there's a kitten miaowing
with soft fluffy fur
or maybe there's a unicorn
with a glittering horn
staring into your eyes.

Go and open the door.
Maybe there are soft snowflakes
falling to the floor.
Maybe there's a salty ocean
with glittering blue water.
Maybe there's a rainbow
with coloured arched doors
or maybe there's a shimmering moon
with light that shines in the dark night.

Go and open the door.
At least there will be light.

Abigail Biggs (8)
Pitsford Primary School

Beyond The Door

(Based on 'The Door' by Miroslav Holub)

Go and open the door.
Maybe there's a glittering treasure box
waiting to be opened.
Maybe there's white snow
covering the whole world.
Maybe there's a moon
glimmering down at you
or maybe there's a bright star
falling to the ground.

Go and open the door.
At least there will be
something new.

Daniel Collins (8)
Pitsford Primary School

Crocodile

I see a crocodile
Hunting for its prey,
Sneaking on four legs.

Its dark green,
Hard bumpy skin
Covers its body
That's long and lean.

As he opens his jaws
Hiss, hiss.
Watch out!
It thinks you're dinner.
Careful . . .

Matthew Chamberlain (7)
Ringstead CE Primary School

My Dolphin

I see a dolphin splashing
Playing in the water
Catching fish
And eating them.

Doing a backward flip
Over a boat
Then diving.
Skin smooth like leather.

I hear it talking to me
This one's a champion
Here it is
Looking at me.

Frances Talman (8)
Ringstead CE Primary School

My Dolphin

I see a dolphin
Splashing in the water
Catching fish
And eating them.

Doing a backwards flip
Over a boat.
Going swimming
Near the boat.

It is splashing
In the sea.
Looking at me.

Ellie Defries (7)
Ringstead CE Primary School

My Horse

It is in a race
It is running
Like a racing car.

It has white fur
Like clean snow
Thin like a sausage.

Its fur is soft
Like a teddy
It makes a nibbly sound.

It shows people
How wonderful it is.
That's my horse.

Gemma Hollis (7)
Ringstead CE Primary School

Panda

I see a panda
Eating tasty bamboo.
Moving very slowly,
As black as the night
And as white as snow.

As fluffy as a teddy;
Munching, crunching, grinding
(Is all you can hear when he's eating)
Constantly eating bamboo
That's my panda.

Alec Morgan (8)
Ringstead CE Primary School

Shark

I see a shark
Eating lots of fish
Gliding through the water

I see him
Looking like a rain cloud
His body like an arrow
His body's all smooth

He makes a swooping noise,
When he's swimming.
Eating lion fish, clownfish
And all sorts

When there's a shark
Watch where you swim!

Tom Watton (8)
Ringstead CE Primary School

Big Dog

I see a big dog
Running around the earth
Moving like lightning
Black and white, like a zebra.

Oval, like an egg
Fluffy, like cotton wool.
It barks at people,
I think it's amazing.

Benn Martin (8)
Ringstead CE Primary School

Night

His gentle breath,
sweeter than the song of the birds.

Like a caring brother
he gently wrapped his arms around me.

His gentle, caring face
fading into the light of the lamp.

His gentle deep blue eyes
his soft and velvety clothes
glisten in the night.

Jumping from dream to dream
to make sure everyone has a lovely sleep.

Jack Palmer (10)
Ringstead CE Primary School

Fear

Fear is like a raging volcano, erupting as we speak
Fear is a roaring wave, crashing on the beach.
Fear is silence with no end.
Fear is like a dark night with no dawn.

Fear is a forever sad evening, with no conclusion
Fear is blood dripping.
Fear is like death but never-ending.
Fear is danger behind you.
Fear is hunger with no food.
Fear is hate with no love.

William Westall (11)
Ringstead CE Primary School

Gubly Goop

Hubble bubble,
Bedroom trouble,
T'Vs on and lots of rubble.

Sim card of a mobile phone,
Chocolate flake of an ice cream cone.

Too much traffic causing collision,
A pair of glasses to help my vision.

Empty beer can from the pub,
A hot tap from the tub.

Broken monitor of a PC,
A new window but no key.

A house made from some sticks,
3 chocolate bars, make it six.

A rusty old spoon in the sink,
Some coloured pencils, but no pink.

For a spell of crazy muddle,
A potion from Hell won't give you a cuddle.

Andy Lees (10)
Ringstead CE Primary School

Flower Power

Flowers, flowers everywhere
Flowers soaking up the sun
Flowers, flowers with extraordinary powers.

Pink, red and a whole lot more
Sparkling and sizzling in the summer's sun.

So that's a flower with mind-blowing powers.

Katie Surridge (11)
Ringstead CE Primary School

Dreammaker

Night was looking at me peacefully,
Watching my every move.
Coming closer and closer,
Swiftly but slowly.

Her hair flowing over her face,
She whispered in my ear
The dreams I long to hear.

Her face shining like the moon,
Glowing through my window.
Her eyes glittering like the night sky.

As she left me silently,
I fell asleep peacefully.

Gemma Horton (11)
Ringstead CE Primary School

My Puppy

I see a little puppy eating his lovely dinner.
He's got a tiny tail.
He's as black as a witch's cat.
He's fluffy like a summer's cloud.
He barks and whimpers.
He runs with his tail,
Under his bottom.
That's my puppy, the best one ever.

Natalie De Quincey-Wykes (8)
Ringstead CE Primary School

The King Of Night

(Inspired by 'I Met at Eve' by Walter de la Mere)

I met at eve the king of sleep
As lonely moss forms his lovely name.

Thou travels through the hush of wind,
House to house he creeps with pearl-green eyes
He peeps at children's dreams.

His stainless white tunic, florescent in the pitch-black sky,
His golden curls so soft like a pillow.

His face smiles like a tulip greeting the sun.
His life of gold in his night-black home.

I met at eve the king of night,
As lonely moss forms his lovely name.

Christian Brigginshaw (11)
Ringstead CE Primary School

My Parrot

I see a parrot.
Eating berries from the ripening bush,
Flying everywhere looking to land.
Red, blue, gold and green like a rainbow glistening in the sun.
Sleek and long is the shape of its body.
Its feathers are fluffy like a teddy.
Squawking and squawking, speaking to each other.
Looking out for other animals.
That's my fluffy parrot, he's come and landed on me!

Thomas Lees (9)
Ringstead CE Primary School

What Is Anger?

Anger is a hot match that never goes out.
It is the dark red blood on a sharp dagger.
But what if anger is a boiling pot of hate?
But what if it's a raging train?
I'll never know.

Michael Towers (10)
Ringstead CE Primary School

The Sea

The frothy waves bolt through the air,
The rocks demolished by the fierce waves,
The smooth sand tumbling over the rocks,
Wild tigers striking through the foamy tide of the waves.

Ryan Lacey (11)
St Mary's CE Primary School, Burton Latimer

My Sea Poem

The sea with almighty waves and fluffy foam,
Violently crashing against the rocks,
Rushing towards the sand,
Deadly waves follow, destroying without hesitation.
So beautiful as it shrinks and floats back from the beach.

Ethan Field (9)
St Mary's CE Primary School, Burton Latimer

The Sea

As the calm water begins to churn, it grows into a big storm,
Waves start to eat at rocks,
Frothy foam fires everywhere,
Waves rage with power,
Rocks get obliterated to the power of water,
Ripples on the water increase into an invincible whirlpool,
The water opens its mouth to devour a rock,
Sand sprays everywhere and settles onto the bottom of the sea.

Kade Purbrick (10)
St Mary's CE Primary School, Burton Latimer

The Sea

It's amazing how the fearsome waves
push towards the shore,
they jump out and grab the rocks
leaving stones falling.
The golden sand getting snapped shut into its jaws.
Salty seawater spraying everywhere.
Snakes striking out fearsome venom.
Suddenly everything's asleep and calm.

Chloe Baugh (10)
St Mary's CE Primary School, Burton Latimer

The Sea

The whooshing waves fly past,
Sometimes the sea is silent,
But is never still,
The rustling rocks crash and crumble,
Bubbly bubbles.

Annie Wilkinson (10)
St Mary's CE Primary School, Burton Latimer

The Sea

Waves clashing against the rocks,
Foamy feel,
Breathing breath as strong,
Energetic sea causes hyper waves as they meet.
Eating the rocks as they speed.
Knocking over sandcastles,
Holding onto its energy,
Going completely wild,
Giving great knocks,
To all rocks.

Elena Attfield (11)
St Mary's CE Primary School, Burton Latimer

The Sea

What a beauty the sea can be, calm or wild.
Waves bash rocks till they crumble and shatter.
White horses charging through the sea.
Froth spits up.
The forceful froth appears like a watery fire.
The lashing noise is deafening.
The wind is lashing against the big huge cliffs.

Hannah Rose (11)
St Mary's CE Primary School, Burton Latimer

The Sea

Whistling white waves soaring through the rocks,
Crumbling golden sand turning into land,
Splashing, salty sea envious of the swimmers,
The calm sea drawing to the sand,
Foam slamming against the cliff back.

Maisy Smith (11)
St Mary's CE Primary School, Burton Latimer

The Foundation Of The Ocean

Bursting, banging
Roaring rocks
Whistling, whittling
Soaring drops
Deafening, dooming
Dangerous waves
Frightening, falling
Thundering sprays
While shouting and stomping
Swinging and raising
The foundation of the ocean.

Alysha Kassam (9)
St Mary's CE Primary School, Burton Latimer

Sea Poem

Storms occurring, winds blowing
Deferring waves, stones shattering,
Boom! Boom!
Waves eating rocks
Smash! Smash!
Foam bubbling over the rocks,
Splash! Splash!
Rain falls, sea grows
Plop! Tap!
Winds blowing harshly
Sssssssshhhhhh!

Adam Tattersdale (10)
St Mary's CE Primary School, Burton Latimer

The Sea

The wild waves whoosh crumbling rocks,
ripples rage as they run through the sea
until they reach the shore.
The spraying foam gets lifted up high with the waves
then slowly the waves are whirled away.
Suddenly the power is taken away as if by magic.
Then everything is still as it sleeps.
But then galloping white horses glide across the sea,
ready to start another fight.

Danielle Reeve (11)
St Mary's CE Primary School, Burton Latimer

The Sea

A roaring wave drooping with frustration,
Waves like bowling balls,
Striking out with a spitting frothy foam.
An aggressive, breathless burst of energy,
Scattering rocks everywhere,
It's a bubbling, beautiful sight!

Hannah Gurney (9)
St Mary's CE Primary School, Burton Latimer

The Sea

A herd of screaming grey horses hitting the rocks.
Crashing white tigers, fierce and wild.
Hissing snakes, angry, brave and spitting.
The sea, strong and stormy.

Layla Lindsay (10)
St Mary's CE Primary School, Burton Latimer

The Sea

The ravenous sea leaps at the fearful foam,
White horses gallop in the breeze,
It seems to move towards the frightened foam,
Shouting as loud as thunder,
Fierce, frustrated waves wail in the wind,
The fearful foam flutters onto the resting rocks,
All is quiet, safe at last.

Anne Grey (10)
St Mary's CE Primary School, Burton Latimer

Waves

Waves bashing against the rocks.
Boulders cracking, big waves
Spinning into the sand.
The waves charging with anger.
The sand left drenched,
Waves still bubbling with rage.

Conor Sellers (10)
St Mary's CE Primary School, Burton Latimer

The Sea

The sea makes the nicest sound ever.
Crashing waves attack the cliff.
The huge tide is as tall as mountains.
Powerful waves!

Jacob Bryan (9)
St Mary's CE Primary School, Burton Latimer

The Sea Emperor

Shining droplets soaring through the salty air.
Ecstatic spray lapping up from the ocean floor.
Raging waves, curling their tendrils around a cliff face.
Water hurling rocks at sailing ships.
Crashing foam blasting its strength enviously against the soft sand.

Andrew Winebrenner (11)
St Mary's CE Primary School, Burton Latimer

Crashing

Waves crashing against the pier.
The sprinkling water rising above the rocks.
The waves raising their voice.
Waves left wondering.

Taylor Robinson (10)
St Mary's CE Primary School, Burton Latimer

The Sea

Heavy waves.
The sea opens its hand and grabs at the rocks.
Wild white horses gallop through the frothy swift sea.
This is why I love the sea!

Danielle Evans (10)
St Mary's CE Primary School, Burton Latimer

The Waves

Splashing white waves,
Hitting the hard rocks,
Whistling, soaking water,
The water sparkling on a hot summer's day,
The sea striking its prey, taking it down,
How many fish are in the sea?
Nobody knows.
How much salt is in the sea?
Nobody knows . . .

Nicholas Shelford (10)
St Mary's CE Primary School, Burton Latimer

Splashing

Splashing water waking the rocks,
Pebbles getting smoother by the second,
Water rushing through the sand,
Crabs thinking, *what's going on?*
Poking their heads out of the water
And getting washed away.

James Southcombe (10)
St Mary's CE Primary School, Burton Latimer

The Sea

The sea goes whoosh and clings and clangs.
The waves rampage down the sand.
A crash and a bang, the rocks get hit.
The waves hit a boat like a boy is throwing his toys around.

Matthew Bull (9)
St Mary's CE Primary School, Burton Latimer

The Ocean

Water cascading
through the pebbles.
Scattering foam.
Crashing against the rocks.
The spray,
constructs its voice.
Whistling waves,
left in thought.

Caprice Bale (9)
St Mary's CE Primary School, Burton Latimer

The Sea

Water crashing through the rocks.
Rocks dripping on the sand.
Sand falling into the water making a yellow colour.
Pebbles falling to the bottom of the sea.

Corina Bulita (9)
St Mary's CE Primary School, Burton Latimer

The Sea

Sprinkling water hitting the rocks,
Dashing water rolling on top of the sand,
Seaweed washing up to shore,
Whistling sea from far behind,
Waves going away to create another storm.

Laura Ross (9)
St Mary's CE Primary School, Burton Latimer

Splash

The ocean splashing against the rocks.
Water flying everywhere.
The waves changing, on a rampage.
The fluffy foam spraying
All over the place.

Katherine Davies (10)
St Mary's CE Primary School, Burton Latimer

The Ocean

Shells scattering at the force of the sea.
Rocks crashing against the waves.
Waves stamping through the sea
Only to be pulled back by its anger.
Sea afraid of what it has done.

Joseph Harpur (10)
St Mary's CE Primary School, Burton Latimer

Deafening Sea

The deafening deep sea grinding against the rocks,
the waves overlapping the land,
then gobbling up all leftovers back into its cold soul,
then left thinking what to do next.

Charley Hull (10)
St Mary's CE Primary School, Burton Latimer

Waves

Whistling waves
Kicking the rocks with rage.
Splashing salty sea.
Swinging on the clouds.
Shouting out with anger.
Slamming the pebbles underneath.
Left on its own.

Joanna Chandler (9)
St Mary's CE Primary School, Burton Latimer

Waves

Water and foam slamming against the cliff face.
Foam brushing against the pebbles,
The spray going red-faced with fury.
Crumbling golden sand washed away by rampaging waves.
Lather rides the waves as it overlaps the shells.

Abigail Hillyard (9)
St Mary's CE Primary School, Burton Latimer

The Sea

Whispering wind
moaning at the sea.
Crashing through the rocks in rage,
grinding through the pebbles, anger firing up.
Everything moves out of the way
with fear, left alone at once.

Makayla Rettie (9)
St Mary's CE Primary School, Burton Latimer

Ocean

Rocks crushing through the shells.
Waves swirling through the sand.
Tides clashing in the pebbles.
Birds whistling as they go by.
Deafening seasalt sprinkling around.

Dannielle Ives (11)
St Mary's CE Primary School, Burton Latimer

The Sea

Charging grey horses let out their anger,
Waves lift up like a snake about to strike,
As it hits the rocks, they shatter into a hundred pieces,
Now searching for the sand,
It takes a deep breath as it slips back down softly
And closes its mouth to start over again.

Emily Hall (11)
St Mary's CE Primary School, Burton Latimer

The Sea

Rocks cracking because of the ocean's strength.
Waves crashing against the piers.
Water rushing through the sand.
The wave's rage is so terrifying
Because it breaks giant rocks.

Jordan Anniwell (10)
St Mary's CE Primary School, Burton Latimer

The Sea

It is a mystery why the sea is so beautiful,
with its speeding water,
aggressive spray and strong waves,
causing booming boulders to crash into cliffs,
surfing sand moving from the rampaging waves.

Aidan Cunningham (9)
St Mary's CE Primary School, Burton Latimer

The Sea

Roaring waves thrashing at rocks,
Frothy foam lingering on them with spraying surf,
Making storming sand rage up and rampage on
through the treacherous tide.
Broken rocks trying to stay whole under the pressure
of the merciless waves.

Benjamin Mitchell-Bunce (9)
St Mary's CE Primary School, Burton Latimer

The Ocean

Water powering over the smooth shells
The open waves charging over the rocks
The waves whispering between each other
The ocean.

Libby Wood (11)
St Mary's CE Primary School, Burton Latimer

The Sea

Waves clashing
Mysterious snake-like sounds
Crabs biting
Sea leaping
Merciless waves
Magnificent waves.

Mary Stone (9)
St Mary's CE Primary School, Burton Latimer

The Sea

Water gushing through the shells
The crashing deep sea
Swooping across the land
The sea booming against the rock in anger
The deep sea left thinking.

Charlotte Watkins (10)
St Mary's CE Primary School, Burton Latimer

Loneliness

Loneliness is like a broken heart
with nobody to fix it.
Loneliness is like an upset child
with nobody to care for it.
Loneliness is like a baby calf
being abandoned by its mother.

Jack Shipton (11)
St Mary's CE (VA) Primary School, Kettering

Force

Force is . . .
like the smell of people's clothes burning.
Force is . . .
like the sound of people in pain and crying.
Force is . . .
the colour dark green like suffocating
and gas polluting the world.
Force is . . .
the feeling of someone worrying
over someone they love who's dying.

Nathan Carr (11)
St Mary's CE (VA) Primary School, Kettering

Afraid

Afraid is when you see an angry bully.
Afraid is the smell of smoke from a fire.
Afraid is like the taste of poison.
Afraid is the colour of pure red blood.
Afraid is the parent slapping a child screaming with terror.
Afraid sounds like a baby child screaming its heart out.
Afraid is like the fast beating heart.

Help stop bullying.
Don't be a bully.

Elliott Gillies (11)
St Mary's CE (VA) Primary School, Kettering

Depression

Depression looks like a tired elderly person
who is sitting in the dark on the sofa on her own crying.
Depression is a dark black hole you see
when you are miserable and depressed.
Depression sounds like a poor, hungry, lonely dog
whining for food.
Depression feels like a really sore cut on your hand
but in your heart.
Depression smells like black smoke of a house burning.

Courtney Searle (11)
St Mary's CE (VA) Primary School, Kettering

Forceful

Forceful is a feeling of violence
Forceful is like a rhino charging
Forceful sounds like a lion roaring
Forceful smells like a heart burning
Forceful is the colour red for blood
Forceful looks like power of a bully
Forceful tastes like an orange getting squashed
Forceful looks like an angry bully.

Kuldeep (11)
St Mary's CE (VA) Primary School, Kettering

Loneliness

Loneliness is a child with an empty heart
with no friends or family to care.

Loneliness smells like a mouldy cheese
being eaten by bacteria.

Loneliness is the colour white
of a world with no people.

Philomena Besa (11)
St Mary's CE (VA) Primary School, Kettering

Depression

Depression sounds like the beating of a drum
with the same rhythm over and over again.

Depression smells like a dead body laying on the ground
and a boy just standing there crying.

Depression looks like a dark cave that's never-ending
with blood flooding the whole place.

Tom Bates (10)
St Mary's CE (VA) Primary School, Kettering

Anger

Anger is the song of defeat.
Anger is the bitter taste of medicine running down your throat.
Anger is like the vision of pain and suffering right before your eyes.
Anger is the silent scream of a girl no one else can hear.
Anger is a push from the hand of hatred.
Anger is the colour red, like a fire of flesh and blood.

Charles Angus (10)
St Mary's CE (VA) Primary School, Kettering

Power

Power is red, like a flame burning through wood.
Power feels like a raging bull, smashing your seat.
Power is a fist bursting into your face.
Power sounds like a lion roaring in a distant jungle.

Jamie Cooper (10)
St Mary's CE (VA) Primary School, Kettering

Afraid

Afraid is like an ogre speaking.
Afraid is like your heart beeping.
Afraid is like the Big Brother eye watching you.
Afraid is like a dog coming to bite you.
Afraid is like when you can smell a horrible uncomfortable smell.
Afraid is like a hand trying to drag you along.
Afraid is like your mum in hospital all alone.
Afraid is like someone knocking the door at night.
Afraid is someone who is lost and wants to go home.
Afraid is you in a wrestling ring standing with an 8 foot man.
Afraid is a gang coming towards you.
Afraid is like a face to face lion.
Afraid is like a mansion covered in cobwebs.
Afraid is like a skeleton lying on the floor.

Sonia Bali (10)
St Mary's CE (VA) Primary School, Kettering

Powerful

Powerful looks like the crying of a book
as it's being slammed on the floor.
Powerful tastes like the bones of a skeleton
smacked upon a door.
Powerful is the colour orange
and is like the sun shining on a puddle and making it feel alone.
Powerful sounds like the trembling, terrible tears of a child
with a father coming after them with an echo of a moan.
Powerful smells like the odour of a dead body
that has been left to rot.
Powerful feels like a child being forced to give a bully money
they just haven't got!

Chloe Kingston (10)
St Mary's CE (VA) Primary School, Kettering

Loneliness

Loneliness looks like low trees with no friends.
Loneliness is a deep secret nobody will ever know.
Loneliness tastes like a chilli pepper that will never lose its taste.
Loneliness sounds like a silent world that will never speak again.
Loneliness is a burning candle getting darker as a teardrop.
Loneliness feels like soft scented cotton.
Loneliness is torn up pieces of paper.
Loneliness is a person looking for a way to come out.
Loneliness is a heart that has stopped beating.

Chelsea Lewis (10)
St Mary's CE (VA) Primary School, Kettering

Seasons

Summer is very hot
Near my birthday, I know what I've got.
I love summer days
It means holidays.

Autumn is when conkers fall
People like to find them all.
Schools are changing
People moving.

In winter we sometimes have snow
In towns people are putting lights up. 'Ho, ho!'
That is bright
I stay up all night.

Spring I feel free
I gash my knee.
Plants and animals are growing
Daffodils, bird seeds are sowing.

Alistair Ferrie (9)
Tiffield CE (VA) Primary School

Seasons

Summer is the time when people are lazy
Clouds block the sun and make it hazy
At school it gets hot
Then people drink a lot

Autumn time, days shorter
My friend Ben is ten
The thick mist
Made me break my wrist

Wintertime adults dress warm
When I start to yawn
Then they go out to play
While I lay

Springtime when I get nasty stings
Snow I draw rings
I get cold
I feel old.

George Oddy (9)
Tiffield CE (VA) Primary School

Snow

Snow is white
It is also very light
I have fun making snowballs
Until Mum calls
I have an ice cream
Whilst watching a football team
I would rather play in the snow
Than watch something I don't know.

Charlie Brammer (10)
Tiffield CE (VA) Primary School

Changing Seasons

Flowers are coming up
Such as little buttercups,
Lambs are being born,
Baby rhinos are getting their horns.

I walk up and down the beach,
All I can hear are seagulls that screech,
People's pasties they are taking,
My legs are aching.

One by one the rich leaves fall off the tree,
Wind starts getting blustery,
Leaves are brown, red and gold,
Trees are starting to look tatty and old.

Expect snow,
Big man says, 'Hoo, hoo, hoo,'
Build a snowman, have a snowball fight
Look at the houses, flashing on and off - colour lights.

Tom Hunt (10)
Tiffield CE (VA) Primary School

Racing - Haikus

Fast and furious,
Roaring, amazing, scary,
Push to the limit.

Going very quick,
Raging monsters, at the edge,
Winning or losing.

Tenth of a second,
Makes a great big difference,
Crashes, overtakes.

William Wilkins (10)
Tiffield CE (VA) Primary School

Seasons

Winter
There is so much fog,
I can not get through the bog.
Behind the snowman,
Someone says, 'Ho, ho!'

Spring
The doorbell goes ding-ding,
Then the bird sings.
The daffodil can be small,
Round like the ball.

Autumn
The leaves drop on the floor,
The people open the door.
It's damp,
I want to camp.

Summer
The beach is cold,
Dad is half bald.
The baker makes buns,
The housework is done.

Rona Ireland (9)
Tiffield CE (VA) Primary School

I Have A Green And Red Dragon

I have a green and red striped dragon.
I bought her from the dragon market.
I keep her in a huge bed, as big as a greenhouse
because she's too big for a basket.
Her wings are yellow, green and red,
they look beautiful in the sky.
Her legs are too massive to fit in the house.
She is the only dragon I could find.
When I'm treasure hunting
she helps me dig and find treasure.

Joseph Pady (9)
Tiffield CE (VA) Primary School

Cheesed Off

You wouldn't believe today
So bad I'd rather not say
Because all the cheese
I'm going to wheeze
Was gone, every bit no way

I'd buy a Ford
And become a dark lord
All for a piece of cheese

I'd record a single
With the crunch of a Pringle
All for a piece of cheese

Or paint my shoe yellow
Be a reasonable fellow
And eat it like a piece of cheese.

Andrew Hopes (10)
Tiffield CE (VA) Primary School

Hunting

Time to get up or we'll miss the meet
Groom and wash your pony so she looks impeccably sweet.
Load her in trailer
Go get in the Land Rover.
Here we are, standing around
Giant horses racing around, shaking the ground.
The hounds are excited
Half of them are all excited.
Racing around the countryside
Far and near, close and wide.

Fred Highton (10)
Welford, Sibbertoft & Sulby Endowed Primary School

United Are The Best

Football is fantastic
Football is the greatest
Man U are unbelievable
The best you'll ever see
With Rooney scoring goals
And Ronaldo on the left
It really is a treat
To see them play I say.
With Giggs crossing balls
And Vidic flooding them in
It really is a treat
To see them play I say.
With Van der Sar saving
And Saha shooting
It really is a treat
To see them play I say.

Joe Todd (9)
Welford, Sibbertoft & Sulby Endowed Primary School

Rappy Rap

She rapped on the beach
and she rapped like a peach.

She rapped up and down
and she danced in town.

She rapped in a shop
and she rapped to the top.

As she rapped this is what she said,
'I'm the best rapping gran this world's ever seen.

I'm a slip-slop, trip-trap, happy-happy,
happy-happy, rap, rap queen.'

Sam Baylis (10)
Welford, Sibbertoft & Sulby Endowed Primary School

Little Worm

(Based on 'Today I Saw A Little Worm' by Spike Milligan)

Today I saw a little worm
wriggling on his belly
he just popped up to say hello
and to see what's on the telly
on telly he saw his belly
and wondered what it was
it was ever so, ever so wriggly
and he became the Wizard of Oz.

William Rhodes (9)
Welford, Sibbertoft & Sulby Endowed Primary School

Love

Love is red.
My love sound is *boom, boom!*
It smells like a sausage being burnt.
It tastes like lava.
It looks like it's going to explode.
It feels like when you are in love.
It reminds me of the water in the ocean.

Georgia Bennett (10)
Welford, Sibbertoft & Sulby Endowed Primary School

Happiness

Happiness is a pink spring flower,
It sounds like a tooting flute,
It smells like a wedding rose being tossed,
It tastes like a juicy raspberry,
It looks like a pink spring flower,
It feels like a squidgy foam flower,
It reminds me of my mum surprising me.

Francesca Lansdell (9)
Welford, Sibbertoft & Sulby Endowed Primary School

My Puppy

My puppy is very puffy
I love him very much
He loves my best friend Muffy
He has a very soft touch.

He loves me lots and lots
He crushed my mum's favourite plants
He broke one of my pots
And ruined my brother's pants!

He likes a big cuddle
He makes a big mess
He makes a bigger puddle
As the plants get less and less.

Megan Short (9)
Welford, Sibbertoft & Sulby Endowed Primary School

Guess The Mystery Animal

Long legs
Silent eater
A lone hunter
Speedy creature
African chaser
Big cat.
What am I?

William Boulton (10)
Welford, Sibbertoft & Sulby Endowed Primary School

My Family

My family are different to me
They bounce around upon the sea
They bounce around all day long
They bounce around singing a song.

Dad is big and very bold
Mum is small and very cold
My brother Adam is ever so wild
My baby sister is a little child.

Me, I say, I love to swim
I always, always, always win
I'm very mischievous
And my family are very mysterious.

Sarah Cliffe (10)
Welford, Sibbertoft & Sulby Endowed Primary School

My Magical Bedroom

My bedroom sparkles in the fluorescent light
My bedroom shimmers in the midnight moon
It smells like love and happiness
My bedroom tastes like refreshing fruit
My bedroom looks like comfiness
It feels like lots of magic
My bedroom reminds me of all the lovely things
Like colourful flowers and gorgeous smells.

Amanda Wallace (10)
Welford, Sibbertoft & Sulby Endowed Primary School

Christmas Tree

It's
green, it's
pointy
big and round
it grows
in the
forest
when it chucks
it
down and
it
gets chopped
down
it has
loads
of lights
which are
so
bright
and
a lot of baubles.

Harrison Coltman (9)
Welford, Sibbertoft & Sulby Endowed Primary School

Pancake

P erfect
A roma
N ice
C ake
A lways
K ind to
E at.

Anthony Banks (9)
Welford, Sibbertoft & Sulby Endowed Primary School

Balloons

Balloons can be big
Balloons can be small
Balloons can be short
Balloons can be tall
Balloons can be circular
Balloons can be square
Balloons can be in the shape of a pear.

Balloons can be red
Balloons can be blue
But balloons can be multicoloured too
Balloons can be yellow
Balloons can be brown
Balloons float all around.

Megan Towers (9)
Welford, Sibbertoft & Sulby Endowed Primary School

Mystery Animal

Truly bouncy
So white
Really fluffy
Sweet-smelling
Certainly noisy
Food eater
Doesn't kill
Jumps high.

Mark Hansford (8)
Welford, Sibbertoft & Sulby Endowed Primary School

Monster Down The Loo

Jessie saw a monster down the loo,
She said to her mum, 'It's going to get you!'
It's green and slimy, and has got yellow spots,
And ties its pink ears in double-twisted knots!
It purrs when it's happy and growls when it's sad,
And when it is angry the monster goes mad!
At night he snores and dreams of food,
And if he has a nice dream he's in a good mood!
So that is the monster down the loo,
Beware, watch out, he could be by you!

Harriet Cant (9)
Welford, Sibbertoft & Sulby Endowed Primary School

My Family Poem

My family is a cuddly bear
they keep me in the warm from cold
I sleep in my snug, warm bed
all near where my family sleep
they're always there when I feel alone
every day and night I love my family even more
so let's look at my heart
they're the best family in the world
I love them even more.

Georgia Jones (10)
Welford, Sibbertoft & Sulby Endowed Primary School

The Memory Box

(Based on 'Magic Box' by Kit Wright)

I will put in my box . . .
The smile of a newborn baby
And the hug of a very old lady
The flying fish jumping to the stars

I will put in my box . . .
Lots of fun trapped in a head
No tears falling from sad eyes
Secrets never to be told

I will put in my box . . .
The warm taste of apple pie
Tons of flashing love
And the house that the spirits sleep in

I will put in my box . . .
An eternal flame crackling with a deadly spark
A crack of lightning hitting the nearest tree
And the smile that everyone gives you

My box is made of
Sapphires, rubies and emeralds
And the sparkle of diamonds
Gold, silver and bronze

I will put in my box . . .
Happy thoughts
A genie in a bottle
And the song of the newest robin.

That is what I will put in my box.

Mathew Gay (10)
Welton CE Primary School

A Holiday

The beast sped on until dawn occurred.
A splash of light covered the pavement.
A tower of rocks hugged the road as the car sped on.
What a sight!
What a sight!
The red rocks filled the sky with love
and the dew kissed the car's cheek.

The car coughed and spluttered
as there was not enough petrol
and chugged to the petrol station, panting for breath.
At last a row of petrol holders stood patiently,
as the car skidded to a halt in a slot.

Finally he felt a spark of joy
as his owner pushed and held the petrol holder into his dry mouth.
The petrol shot out like a bullet through the car's body,
as it gave him a last boost of energy for the journey.

A gleaming tower of water caught the car's eye
as he went faster and faster to see what it was.
What was it?
No one knew.
Only the car and his owner.
On a holiday.
A step too fast towards it . . .

Eleanor Bickers (10)
West Haddon Primary School

The West End Wish

The stage is quiet
The lights turn on
The curtains open
As we step on.

We begin to dance
As the music fills the room
The audience is in a trance
As we twirl into the dressing room.

The interval is now
It's time to take a break
It's time to get a cup of tea
And a slice of coffee cake.

The curtains lift up again
The music begins to play
We're going to make the audience gasp
We're going to make their day.

As we take our final bow
The alarm clock begins to ring
I feel like it's all over
But I can't wait for it to begin.

Georgia May (9)
West Haddon Primary School

The Lion - Cinquain

Lions,
Soft, fast, bold, fat.
The lion is fierce and
He eats meat with his dagger teeth.
Vicious.

Daniel Merrick (8)
West Haddon Primary School

Car Crash

The key turns.
The engine roars excitedly.
Its eyes flicker open.
The car has awakened.

Speeding off into the night.
It's looking straight ahead.
But the car has not noticed
What is lurking in the darkness.

Crash! 5, 4, 3, 2, 1.
The car has come to a standstill.
Its owner climbs out, looking for damage.
A scratch, a dent, scraps of paint is what he finds.

Suddenly another monster appears,
Out of the many the car has seen.
But this one is bigger and better the car realises
While being towed out of sight.

Zoë Baker (9)
West Haddon Primary School

The Cowboy

The cowboy was riding his horse like lightning
and came to a screeching halt.
The bandit was wearing brown like a chocolate bar,
he stood still like one too.
Then suddenly the cowboy snatched his gun out of his pocket
and pulled the trigger and shot the bandit like a beat of a drum.
The bandit crashed to the floor.
The people came out of their houses and saw him on the ground.
He crept like a mouse into a corner.
Everybody cheered at the cowboy.

Lewis Bricknell (8)
West Haddon Primary School

The Car Monster

He brushed his sandy feet,
As he left the beach,
Dying of thirst his owner
Walked him to a service station.

After his refreshing drink
They went to a place
That to the monster was unknown,
He was shaking with fear.

Finally he opened his eyes wide
And realised with relief
That they were at a place
With other monsters around.

He eventually got some peace and quiet
And was able to sleep,
But still heard the occasional monster
Waking up to their owners,
Coming back to them.

Carey Davis & Effie Price (9)
West Haddon Primary School

Kittens - Cinquain

Kittens
Always sleeping
Like a baby. No noise!
Sweet and silent. So be quiet.
No noise!

Shh!

Luke Davis (8)
West Haddon Primary School

The Car Monster On Holiday

Crack! The car screamed as he saw some ice.
The ice cracked as the monster skidded on it.
When he got onto the snow,
He almost fell in a pit!

Beep! Beep! Beep! Beep!
The car monster's wheels transformed into blades.
The car raced the skiers down the slope
And he won the race.

He brushed off the snow on his brow
And got out of the wind.
The car was brave and very fearless,
It's such a shame that he was beerless!

The car walked to the restaurant
Where he drank some oil ale.
He sat down for a while and rested
Until his ski blades broke!

Joe Sheen (10)
West Haddon Primary School

Horses

The horses galloped by like thunder.
The grass nice and green, blowing in the breeze.
The big, round, red sun sets in the evening sky.
The sky getting darker as the horses one by one fall asleep,
Peacefully like a purring cat.

Niamh Firth (9)
West Haddon Primary School

The Grizzly Bear - Cinquain

Big bear
Very clever
Hot-headed with sharp teeth
A large carnivorous beast with
Brown fur.

Samuel Ewbank (8)
West Haddon Primary School

Sharks - Cinquain

All sharks
They are so mean
Sharks are tough, rough and mean
Sharks eat fish, meat, dolphins and birds
They're tough.

Imogen Smith (7)
West Haddon Primary School

The Baboon - Cinquain

Baboon
Very clever,
Excellent tree swinger
Never falls down a tree, promise
Me please.

Joe McGrath (8)
West Haddon Primary School

The Bear - Cinquain

The bold
Bear has sharp teeth
His brown coat, it is rough
His sharp and big paws are scary.
The bear.

Heather Mathers
West Haddon Primary School

Dolphins - Cinquain

Dolphins
Are cute and kind
And beautiful. They're blue.
They're wonderful, they have blue eyes.
Skilful.

Sasha Armitt-Warnes (8)
West Haddon Primary School

The Magic Dolphin - Cinquain

Grey, blue,
How about you?
My dolphin is so small
He jumps pretty high. Jumps a long
Way too.

Holly Alder (8)
West Haddon Primary School

The Shark - Cinquain

Big shark
Big grey sharp teeth
Eats fish, big and grey shark
Lives in a salty sea with fish.
Vicious.

Elliott Pugh (8)
West Haddon Primary School

Dolphins - Cinquain

Dolphins
Grey, blue, happy
They are very small, long
They are intelligent creatures
And jump.

Lorna Jolly (8)
West Haddon Primary School

The Horse's Life - Cinquain

The horse
Long, furry tail
Eats carrots and apples.
Lives in a stable made of wood.
Strong horse.

Katie Cope (8)
West Haddon Primary School

Cuddly Rabbit - Cinquain

Cuddly.
Big and bouncy.
Big cuddly, fluffy ears.
Cute and pretty and very soft
Fluffy.

Teedie Brace (7)
West Haddon Primary School

Bunnies - Cinquain

Bunnies,
Little whiskers,
Big floppy ears and a
Little bobtail and soft body.
Bunny!

Annie Sheen (8)
West Haddon Primary School

Big Foot - Cinquain

Big Foot
Has big, big feet.
He is very scary!
He is mean, tough and rough and shy
And tall.

Izzie Kenhard (7)
West Haddon Primary School

Lions - Cinquain

Lions
are camouflaged
and golden. Lions are
furry, grizzly, sly and are strong
and fast.

Holly Mitchell (9)
West Haddon Primary School

Lions - Cinquain

Lions
Are strong and fierce.
Claws are sharp as needles.
They are heavy and have sharp teeth.
They're tough.

Jessica Woodward (8)
West Haddon Primary School

Elephants - Cinquain

Big, huge
and rough and tough.
He is very scary.
He is fat and has big, big feet.
He's mean.

Evie Alder (8)
West Haddon Primary School

The Penguin - Cinquain

Swims fast
Swims for good fish
The emperor penguin
Is the king of the penguins and
Wears crown.

Steven Adair, Ben Stoneman & Indi Armstrong (8)
West Haddon Primary School

The Predator

Great white
looking for its
tea. Then it spots a group
of fish. The shark swims for a fish.
Crunch! Crunch!

Liam Durbin (8)
West Haddon Primary School

Young Writers Information

We hope you have enjoyed reading this book - and that you will continue to enjoy it in the coming years.

If you like reading and writing poetry drop us a line, or give us a call, and we'll send you a free information pack.

Alternatively if you would like to order further copies of this book or any of our other titles, then please give us a call or log onto our website at www.youngwriters.co.uk

Young Writers Information
Remus House
Coltsfoot Drive
Peterborough
PE2 9JX

(01733) 890066